# ARTIST
## TRANSCRIPTIONS
# PIANO

THE KEN WERNER COLLECTION

Transcribed by Joshua Q. Paxton

ISBN 0-634-05735-9

# HAL•LEONARD®
## CORPORATION

7777 W. BLUEMOUND RD. P.O. BOX 13819 MILWAUKEE, WI 53213

Visit Hal Leonard Online at
**www.halleonard.com**

# BIOGRAPHY

Kenny Werner was born on November 19, 1951 in Brooklyn, New York. His introduction to music came at the age of four when he joined a children's song and dance group. At the age of eleven, he recorded a single with a fifteen-piece orchestra and appeared on television playing stride piano. He attended the Manhattan School of Music as a concert piano major. In 1970, he transferred to the Berklee School of Music. There he began to find his creative direction when he met his piano teacher and spiritual guide, Madame Chaloff. Her concept of pulling together spiritual and musical aspects resonated with Werner. This was furthered by his next teacher, Juao Assis Brasil, a concert pianist who successfully demonstrated to Werner effortless piano playing with a self-loving attitude. This ideology continues in Werner's approach to music and creativity today.

In 1977, Werner recorded his first LP that featured the music of Bix Beiderbecke, Duke Ellington, James P. Johnson and George Gershwin. Later that year, he found himself recording with Charles Mingus on "Something Like a Bird". In 1981, he recorded his own solo album of original compositions entitled *Beyond the Forest of Mirkwood*. The following year, Werner recorded the sounds heard coming from his Brooklyn-based studio—a hotbed of late-night jam sessions—and titled the record after his address, *298 Bridge Street*.

In 1984, he joined the Mel Lewis Orchestra. He was beginning to perform more and more in Europe and New York City as a leader and in duos with such notables as Rufus Reid, Ray Drummond and Jaki Byard.

Werner received performance grants from the National Endowment for the Arts in both 1985 and 1987, allowing him the unique opportunity to present his own music in a concert hall setting at Symphony Space in New York. He was also commissioned to compose and conduct a memorial piece for Duke Ellington at St. John of the Divine Church in New York, performed by the Manhattan School of Music's Stage Band and the New York City Choir.

He has also written compositions for the Mel Lewis Jazz Orchestra, now known as the Vanguard Jazz Orchestra. He has since written big band charts for groups such as the Cologne Radio Jazz Orchestra (WDR), the Danish Radio Jazz Orchestra, The Metropole Orchestra (Holland) and the Umo Jazz Orchestra (Finland).

In 1981, he formed his first trio with bassist Ratzo Harris and drummer Tom Rainey. Their first trio CD for Sunnyside records was entitled, *Ken Werner - Introducing the Trio*. He would do another trio album for Sunnyside called *Press Enter* and a quintet album featuring Randy Brecker, Joe Lovano and Eddie Gomez entitled, *Uncovered Heart*. The trio with Harris and Rainey was an association that would last 14 years and record two more albums, *Guru* (TCB) and *Live at Visiones* (Concord). That trio was generally acknowledged as being the most creative, intense and innovative heard in a long time.

The current Kenny Werner trio features the rhythm section of Ari Hoenig on drums and Johannes Weidenmueller on bass. Werner says of these two young players, "This is the first time since Ratzo and Tom that I feel I am featuring a unique relationship, not just a trio." In November of 2000, they recorded a live date from the Sunset Club in Paris. Since that time, they have released three live albums, *Forum and Fantasy* (Doubletime), *Beat Degeneration* (Sunnyside) and the newest release (2004), *Peace, Live at the Blue Note*.

Of the future, Werner says, "I want to lose myself more and more in the bliss of the music. Not only do I benefit from the intoxication, but the audience resonates with their own bliss. In this way, the music wakes us all to who we really are."

# CONTENTS

# All the Things You Are

Lyrics by Oscar Hammerstein II
Music by Jerome Kern

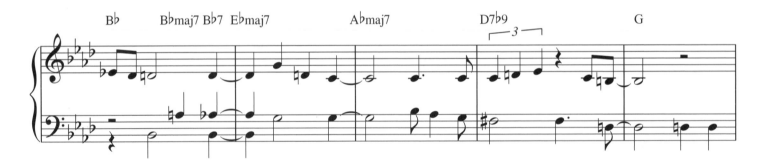

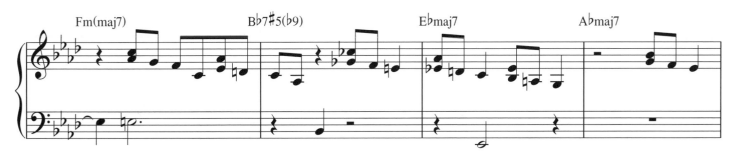

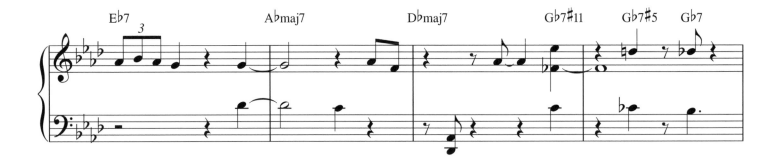

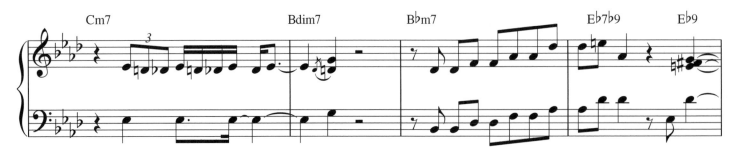

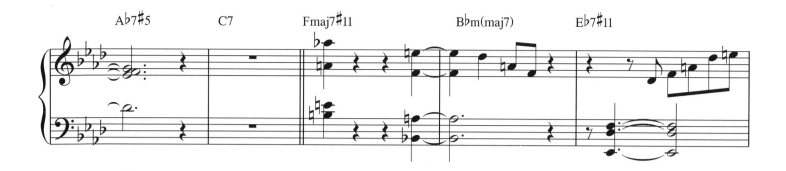

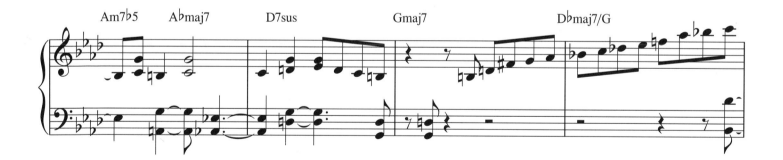

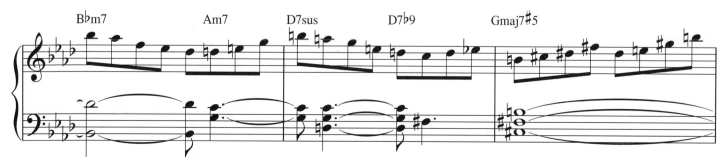

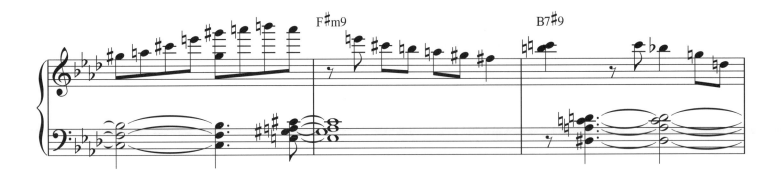

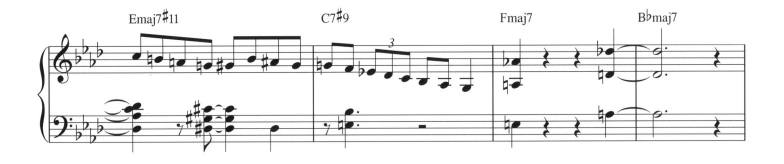

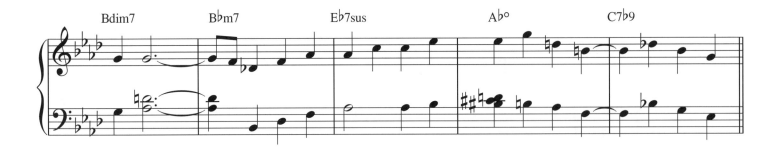

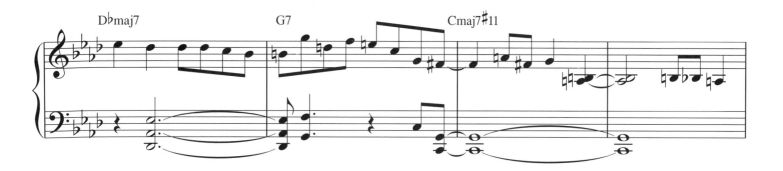

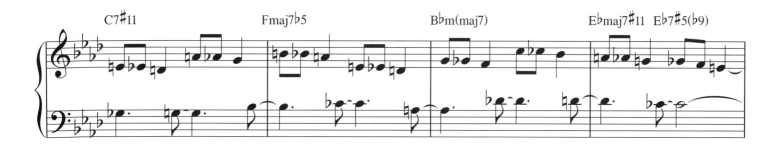

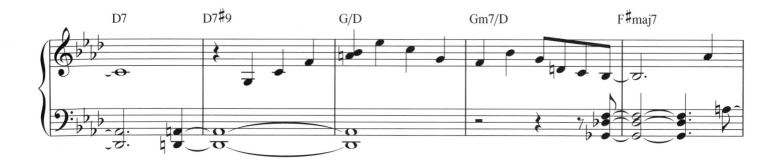

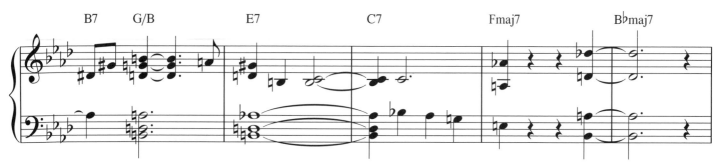

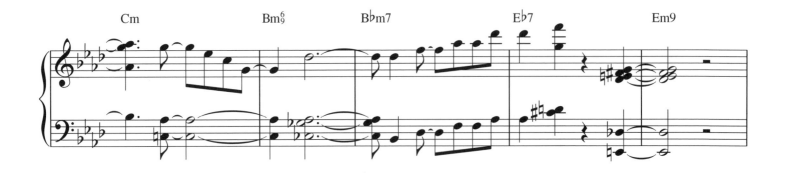

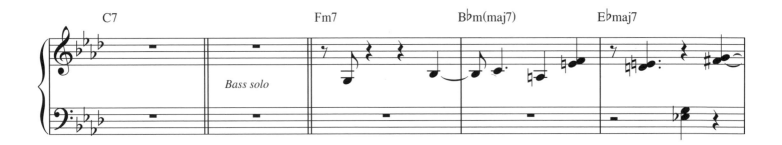

*Bass solo*

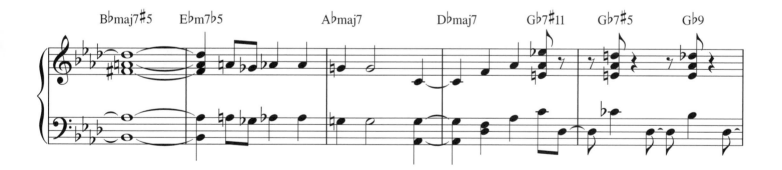

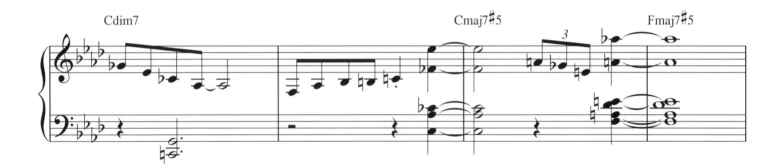

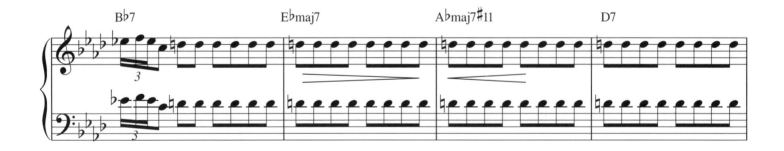

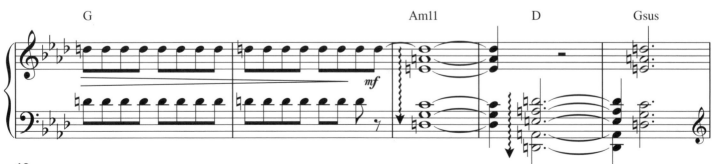

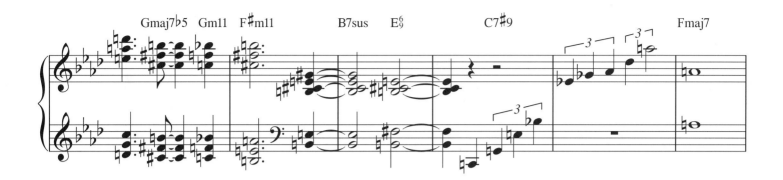

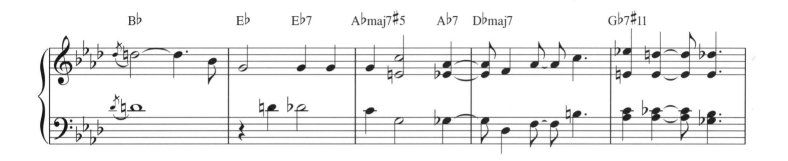

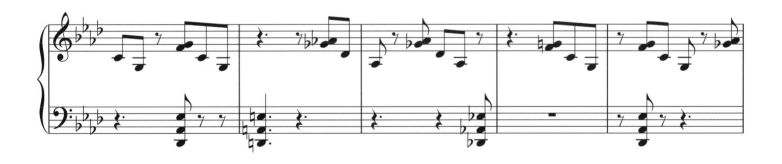

# Autumn Leaves
## (Les Feuilles Mortes)

**English lyric by Johnny Mercer**
**French lyric by Jacques Prevert**
**Music by Joseph Kosma**

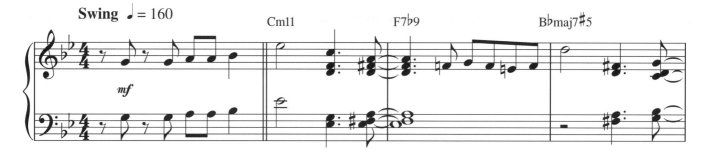

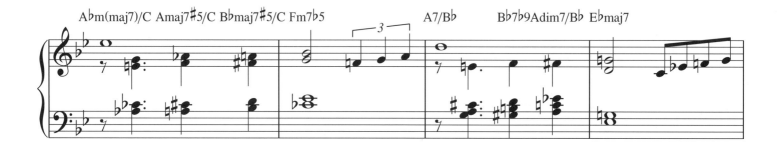

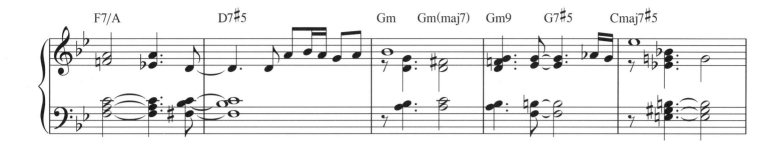

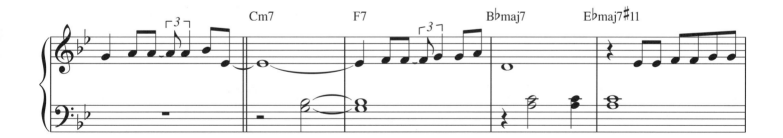

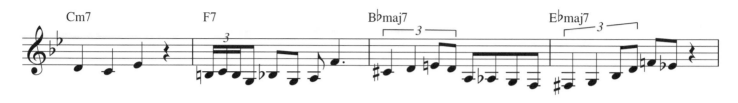

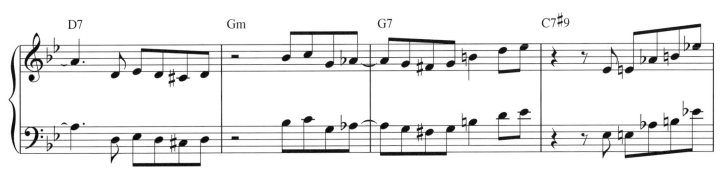

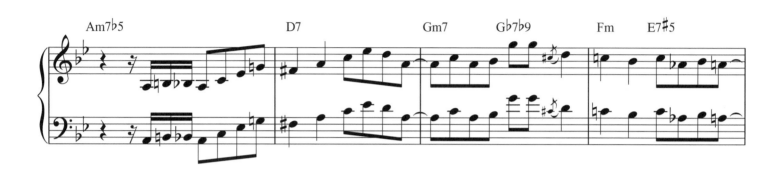

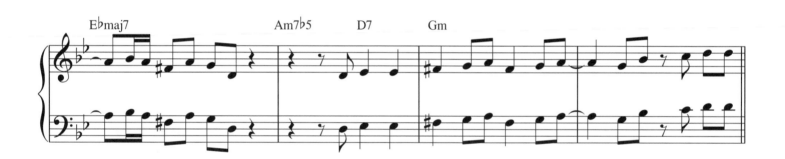

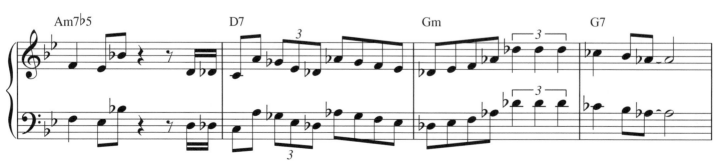

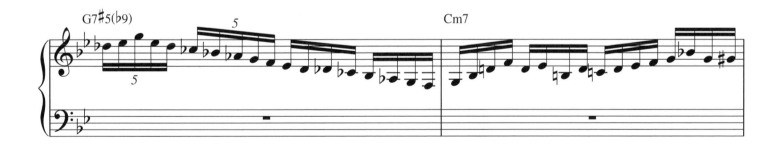

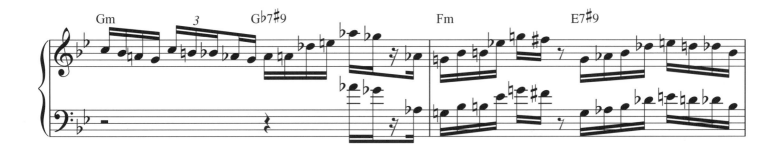

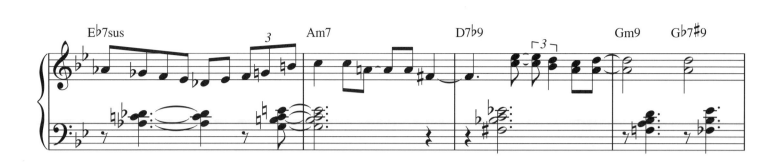

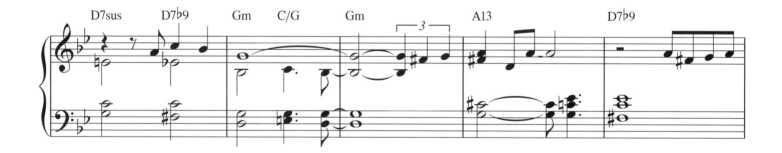

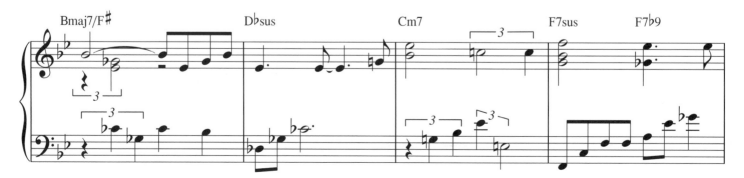

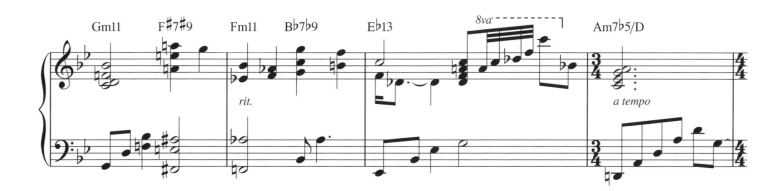

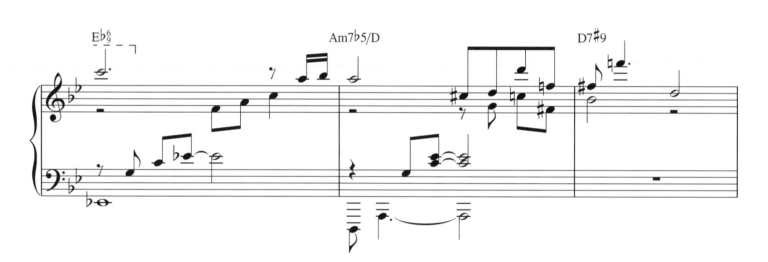

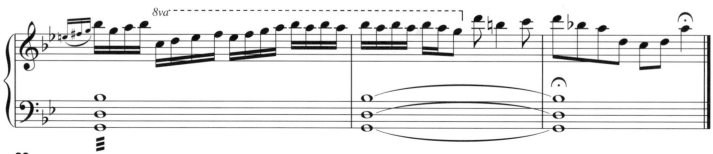

# Blue in Green

## By Miles Davis

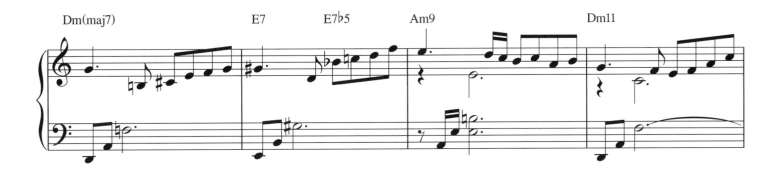

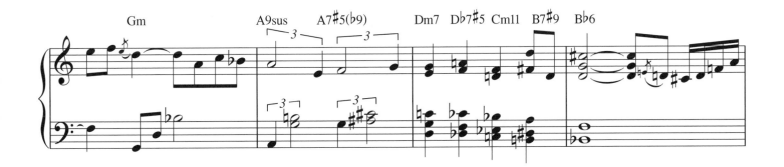

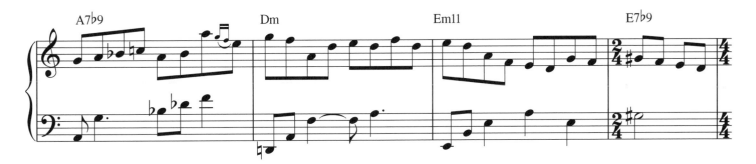

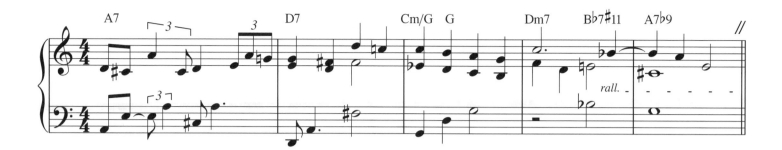

In time ♩ = 135
**Half-time ballad feel**

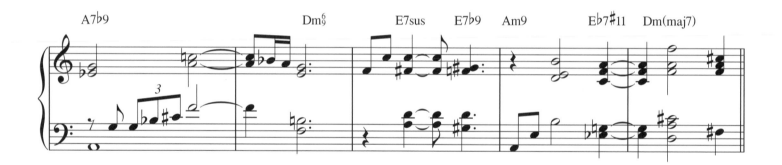

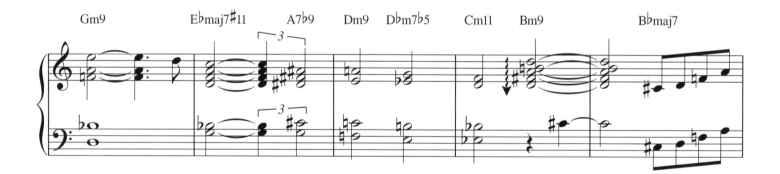

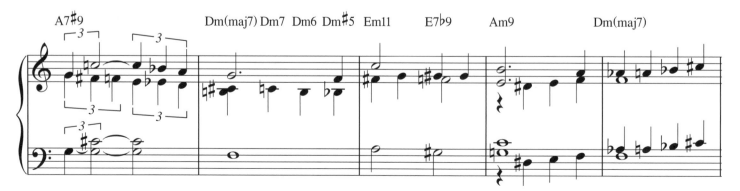

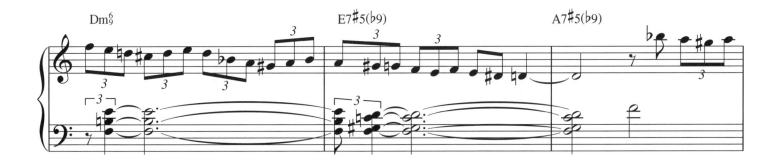

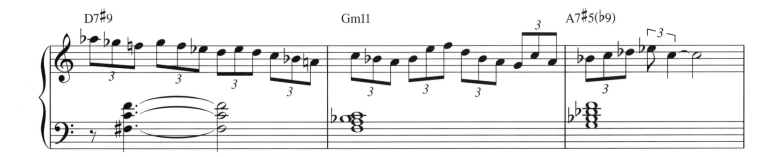

**4/4 Swing feel**

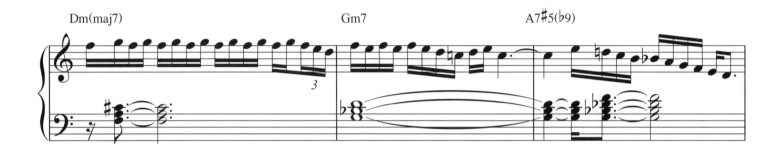

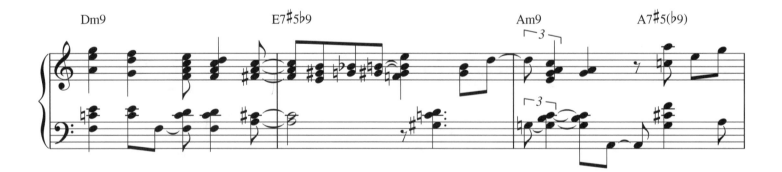

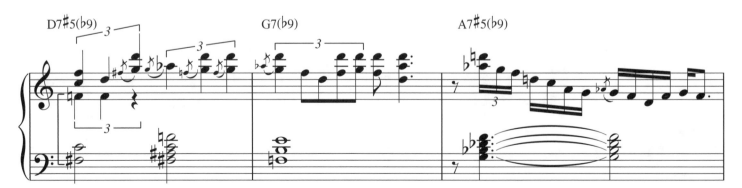

**Half-time Ballad feel**

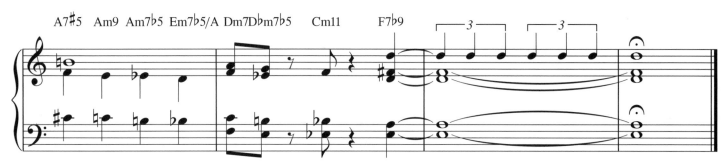

# Ivoronics

By Kenny Werner

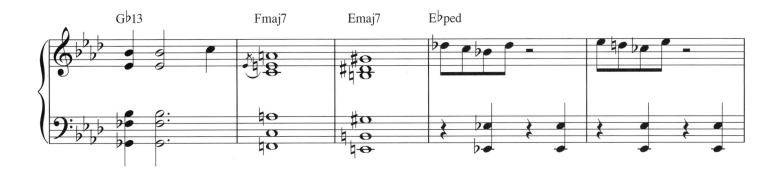

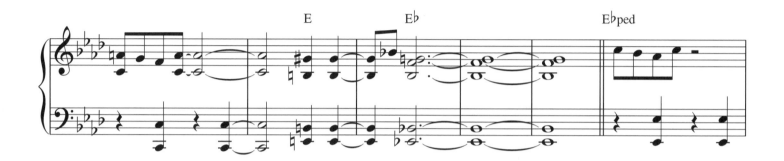

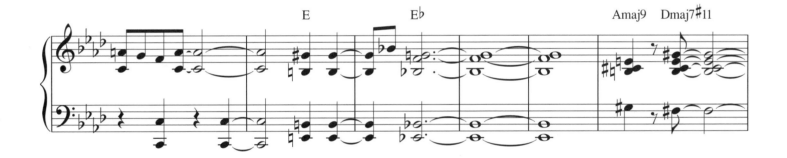

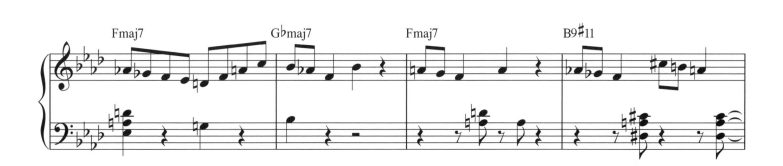

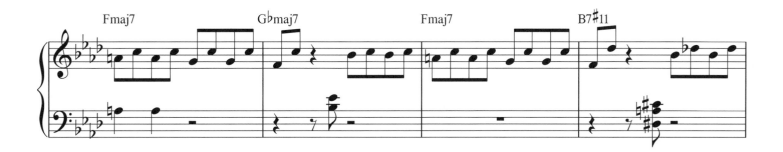

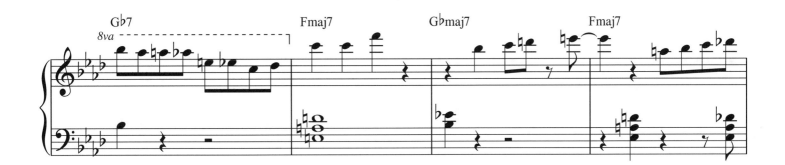

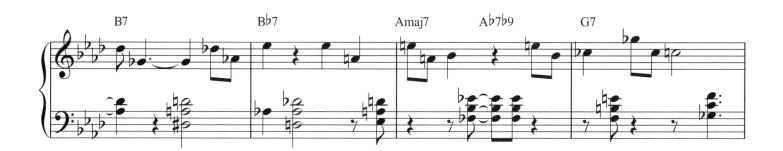

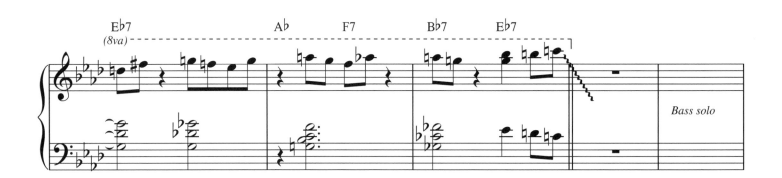

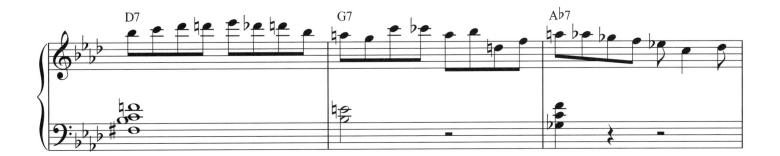

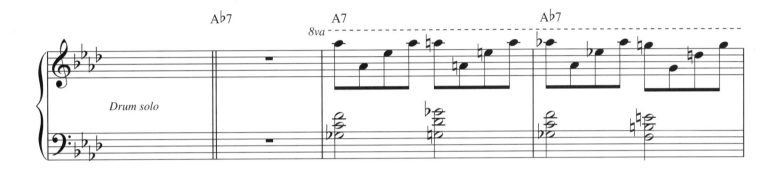

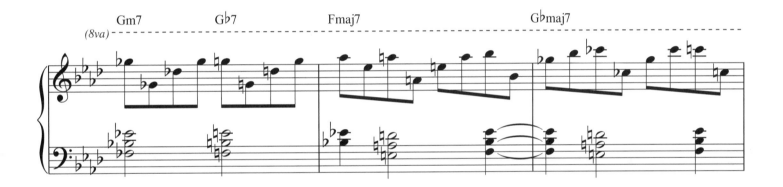

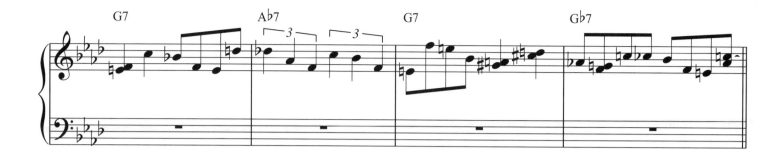

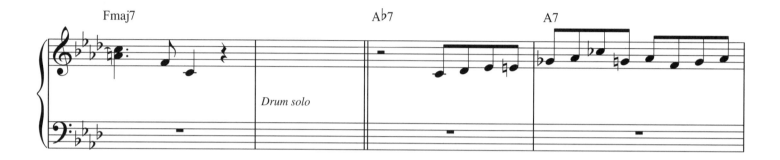

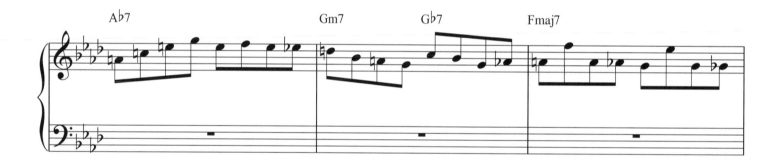

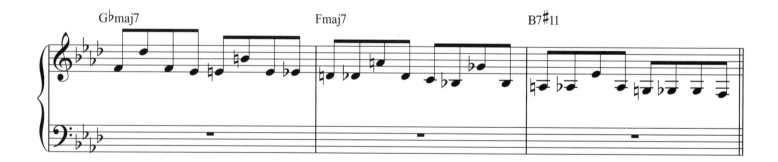

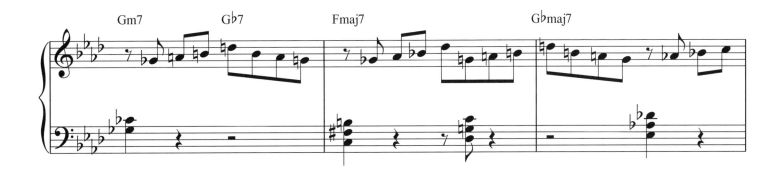

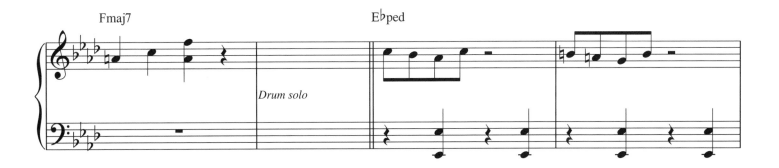

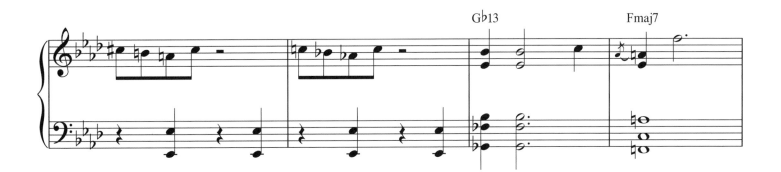

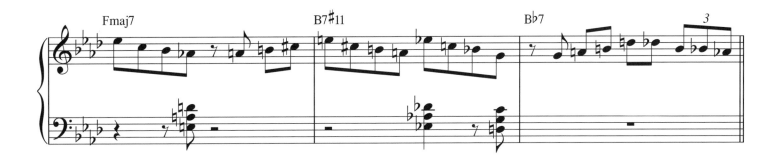

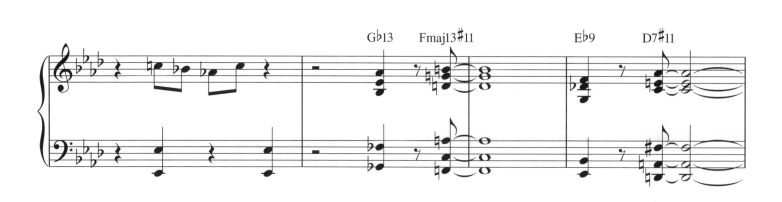

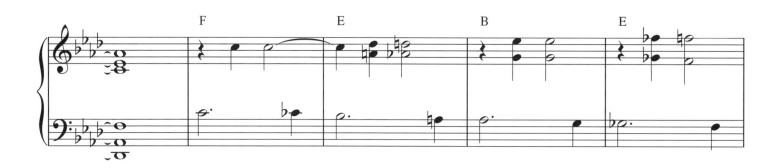

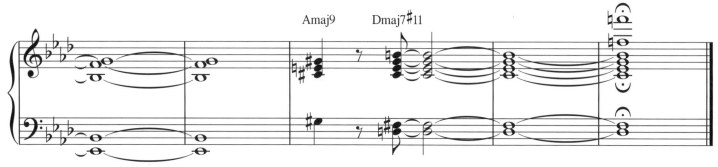

# Little Appetites

**By Kenny Werner**

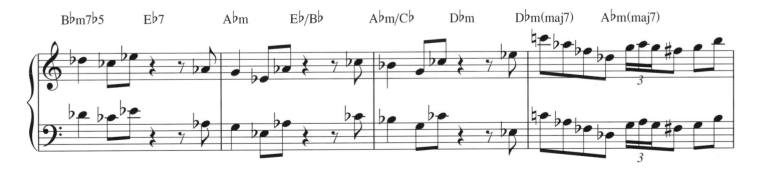

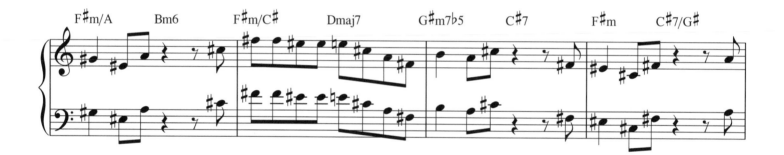

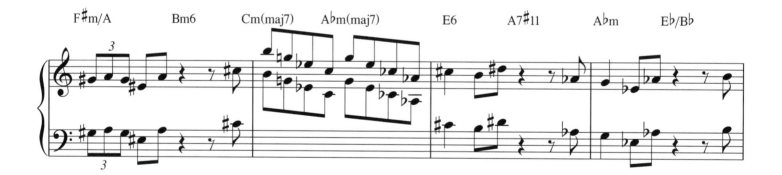

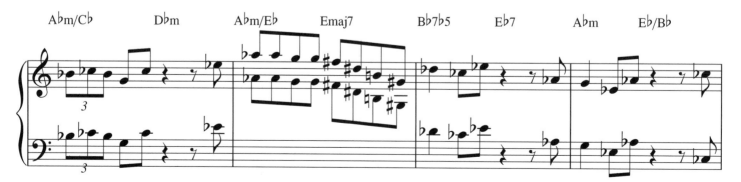

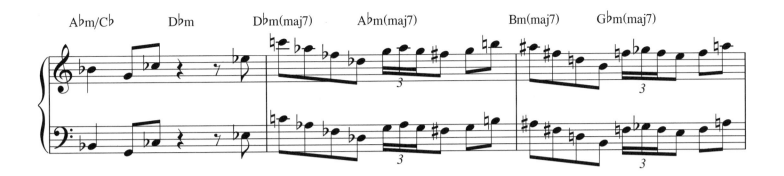

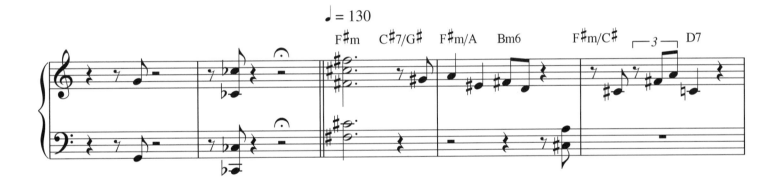

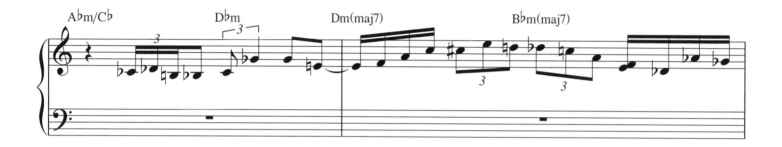

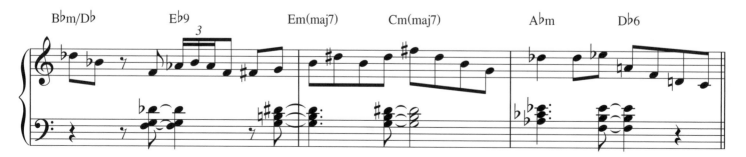

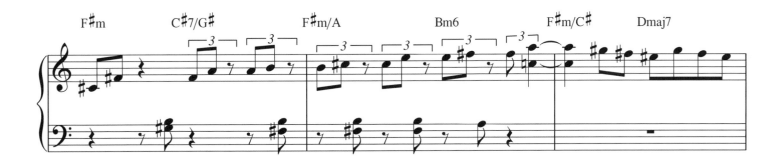

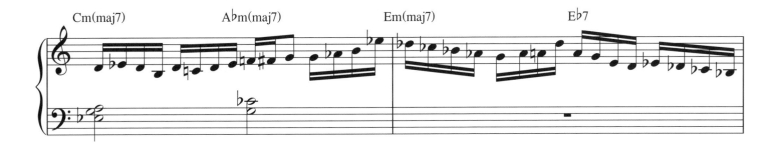

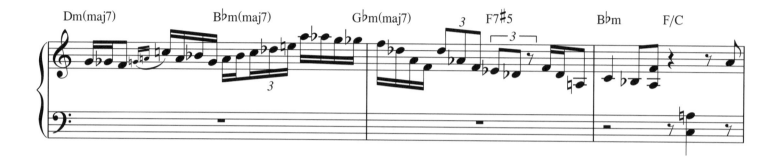

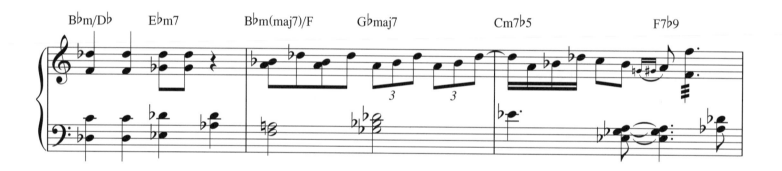

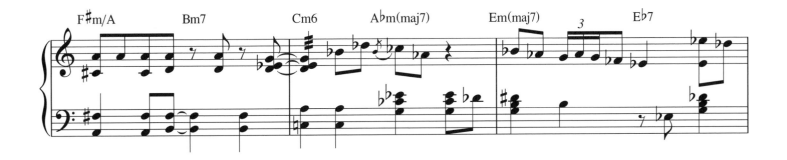

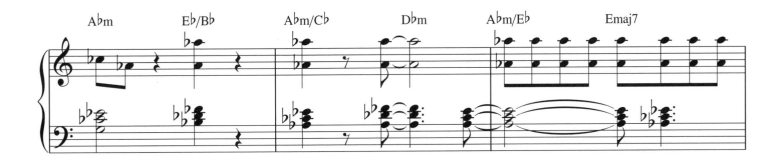

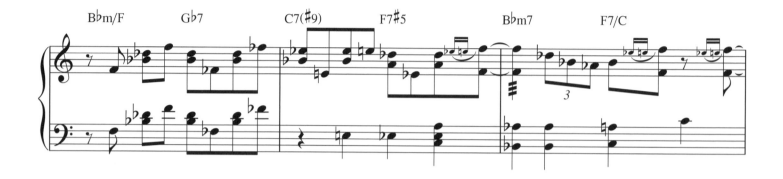

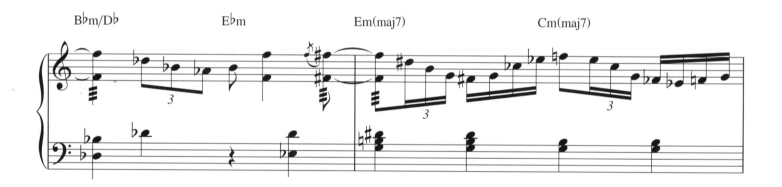

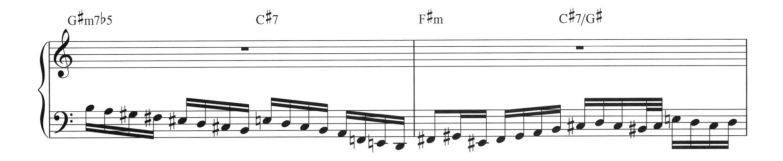

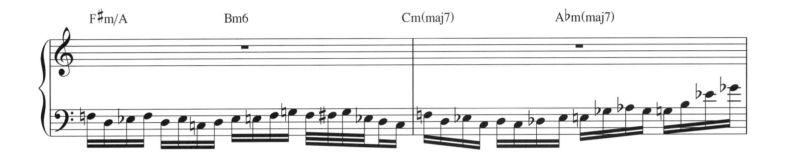

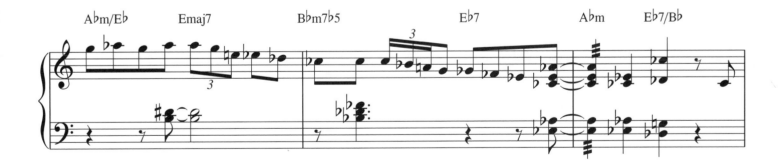

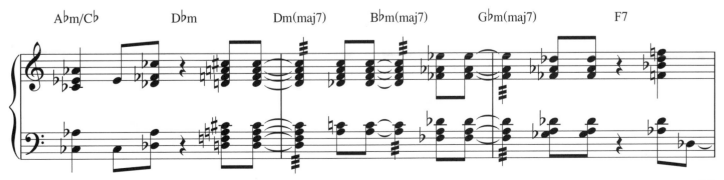

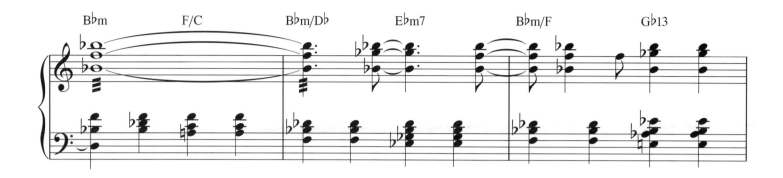

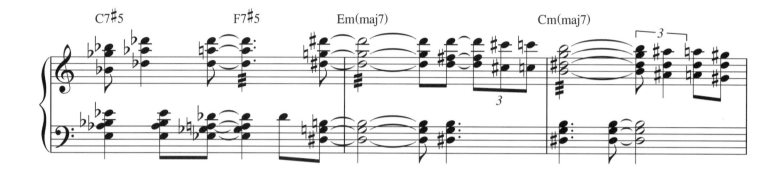

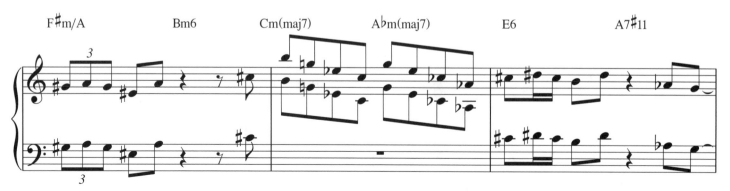

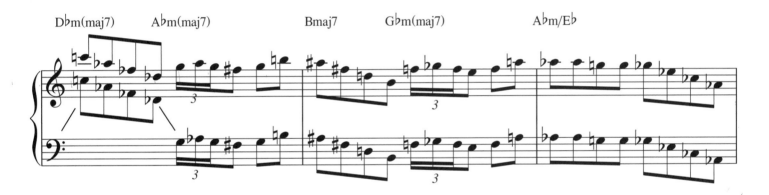

# My Funny Valentine

## from BABES IN ARMS

**Words by Lorenz Hart**
**Music by Richard Rodgers**

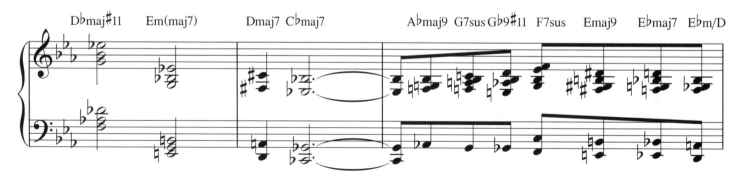

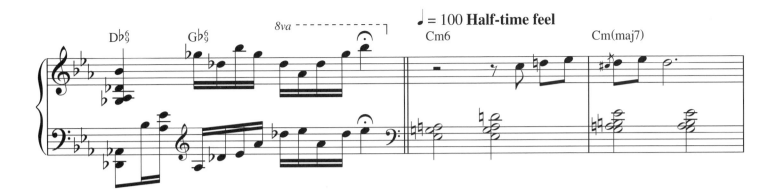

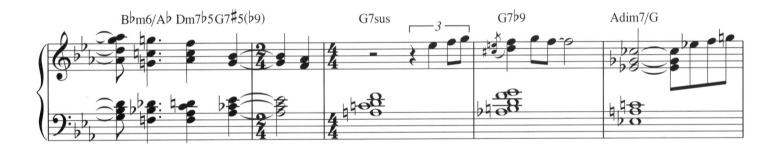

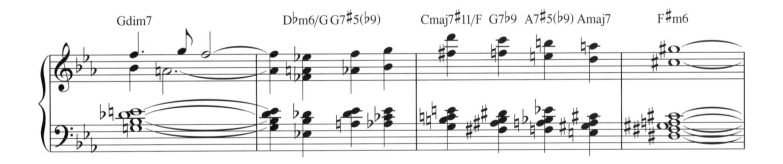

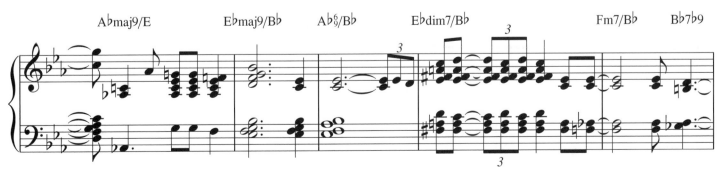

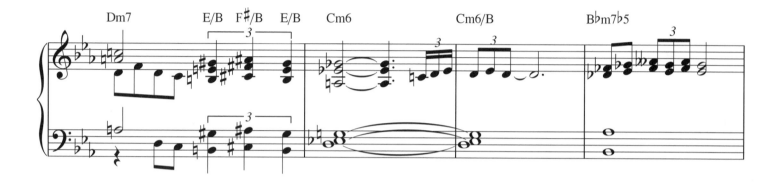

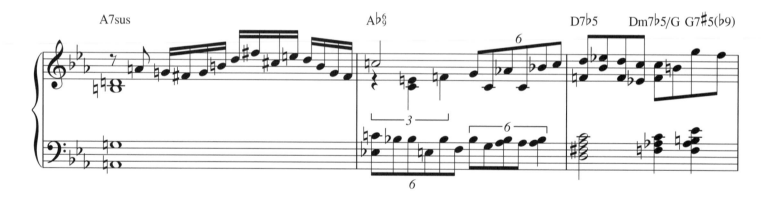

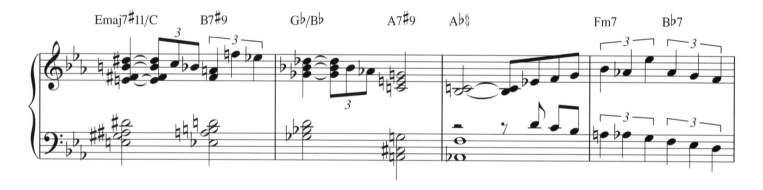

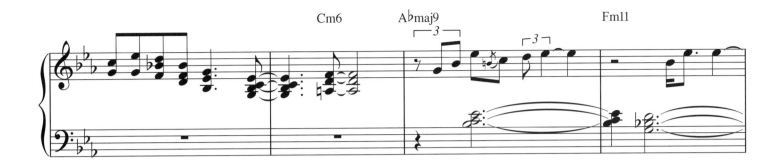

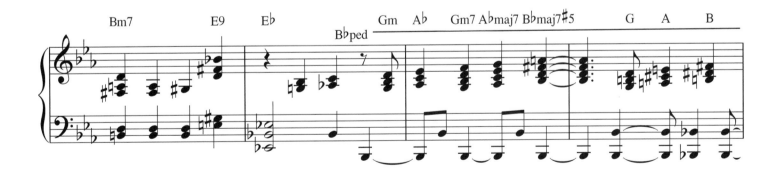

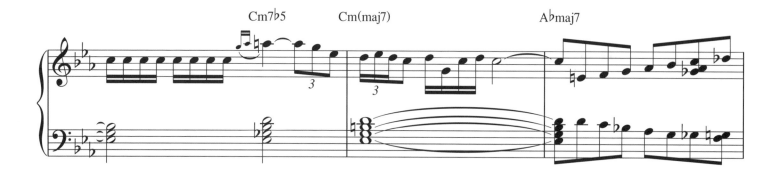

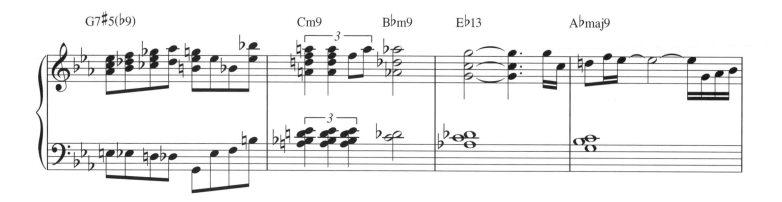

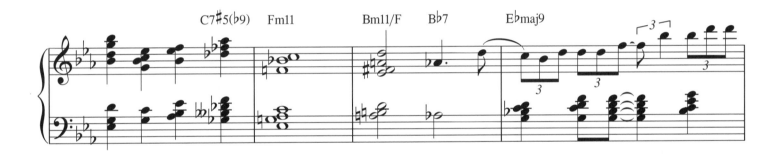

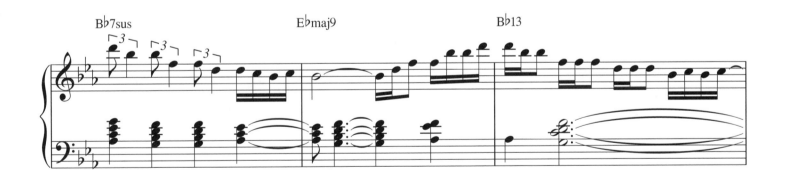

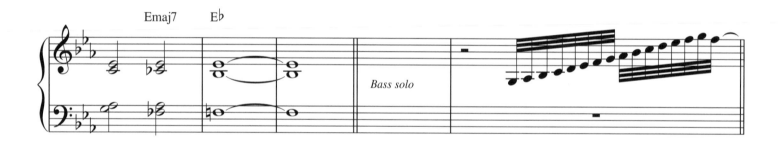

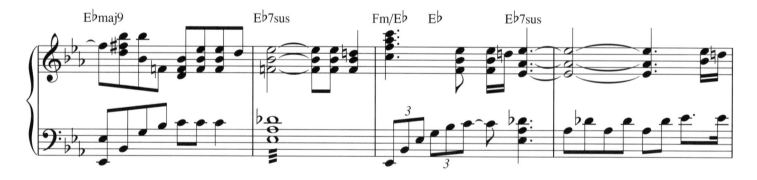

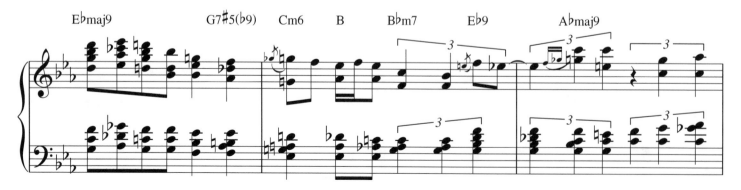

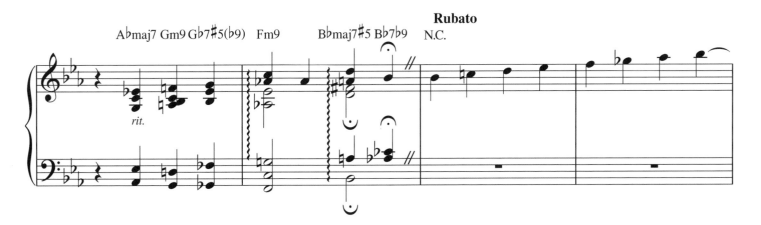

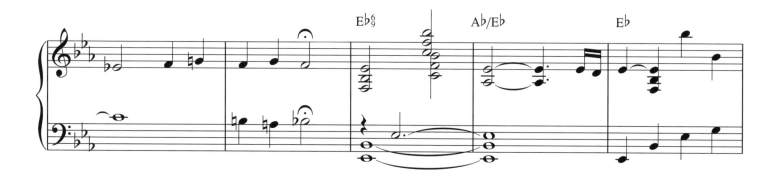

# Nardis

**By Miles Davis**

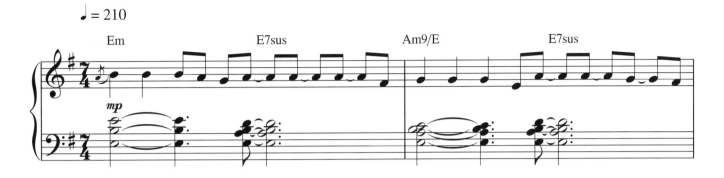

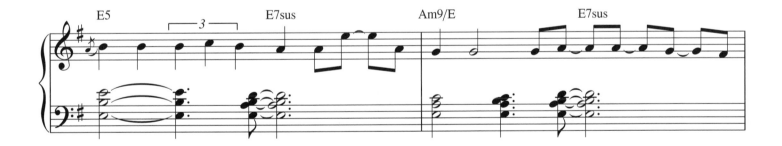

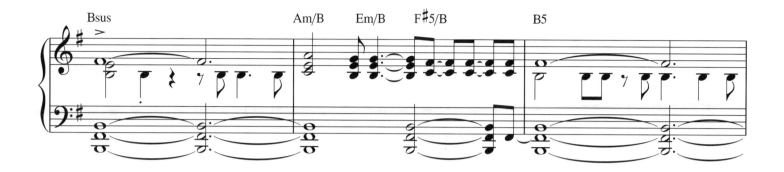

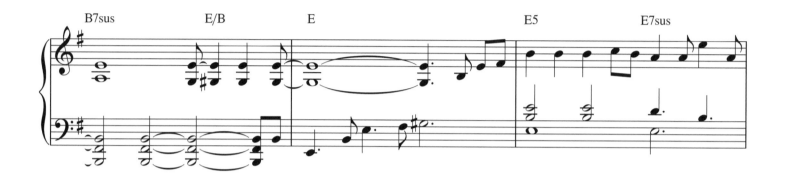

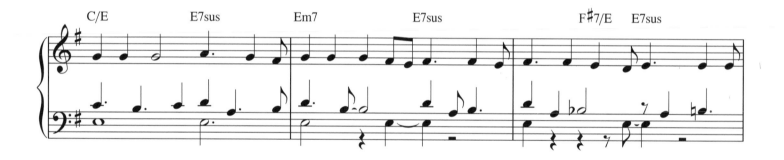

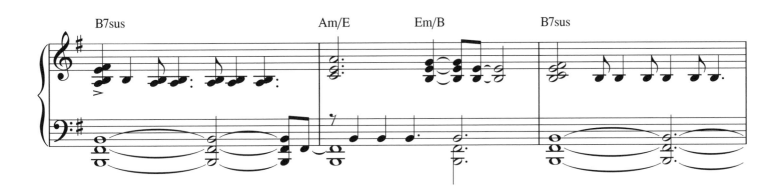

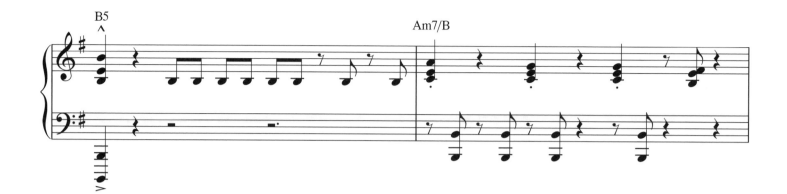

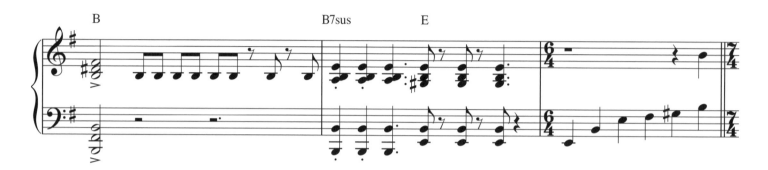

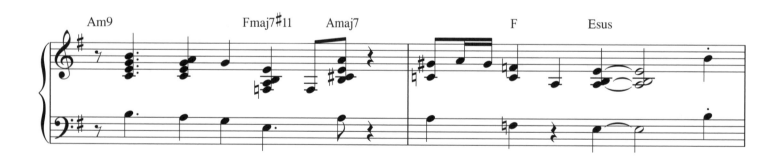

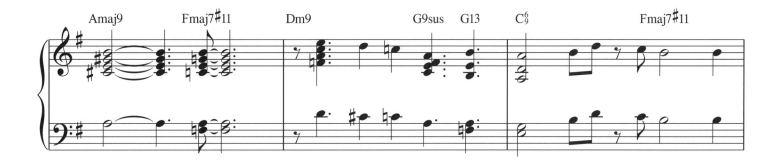

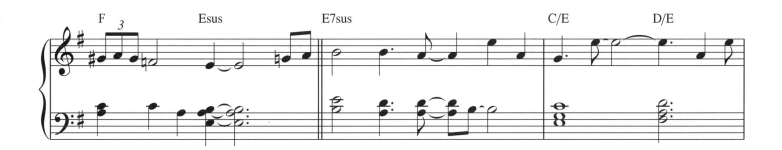

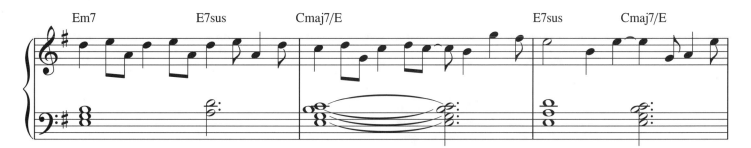

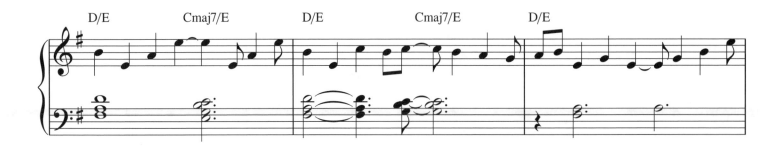

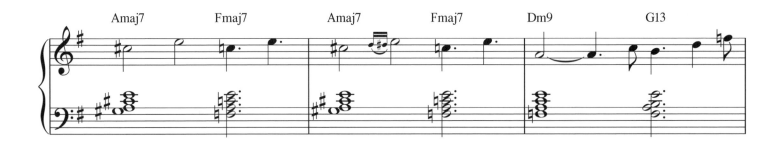

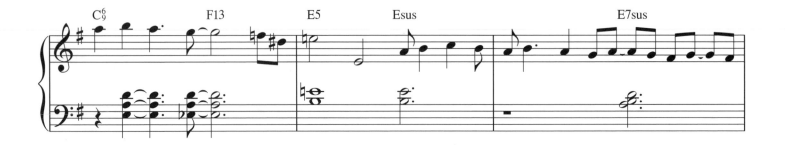

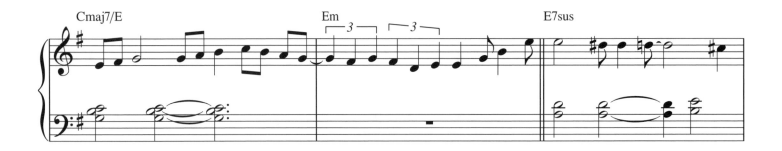

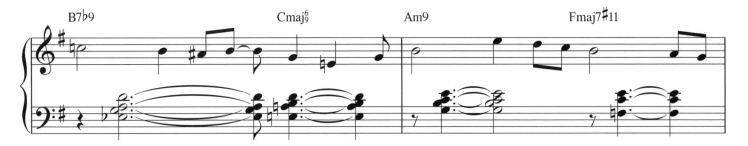

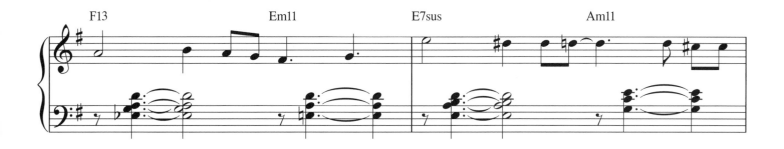

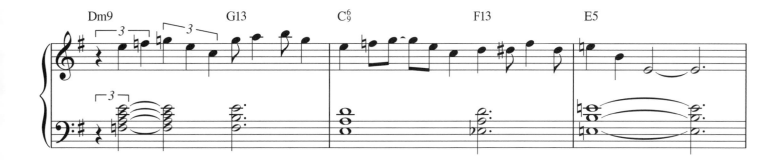

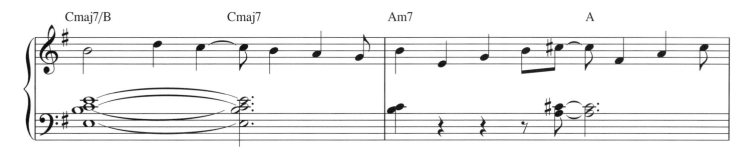

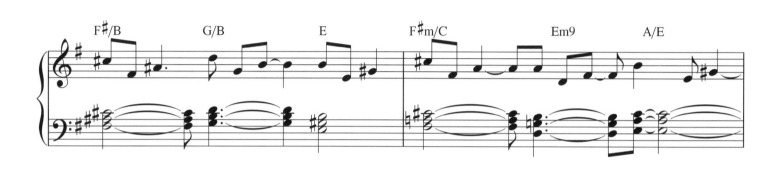

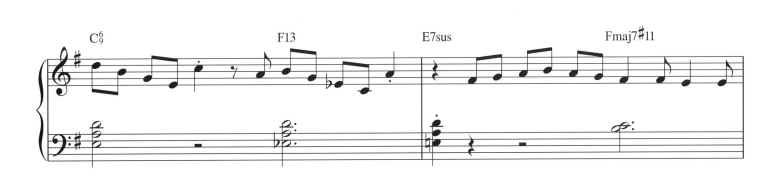

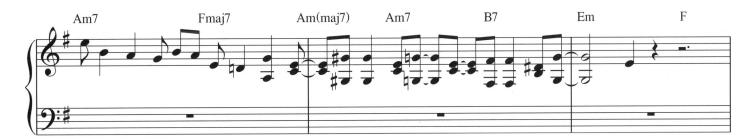

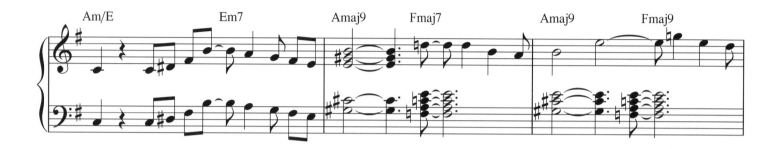

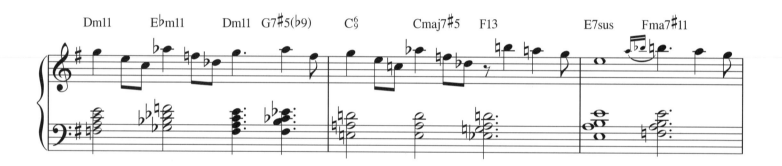

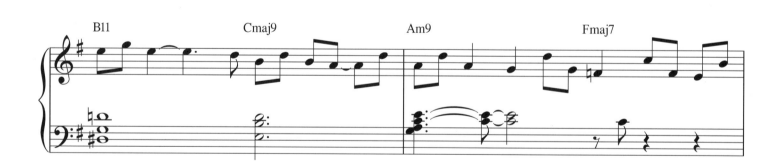

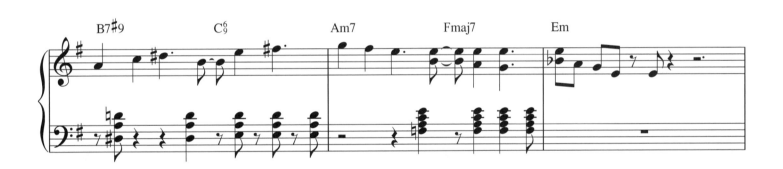

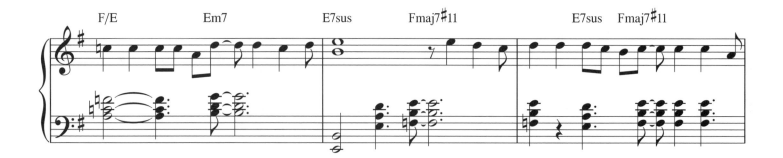

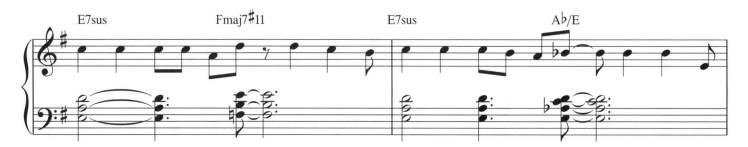

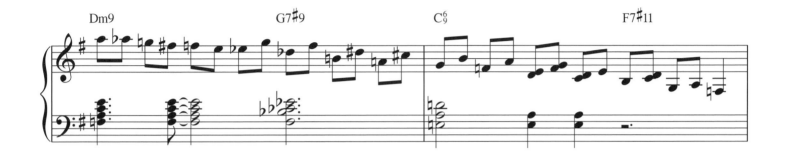

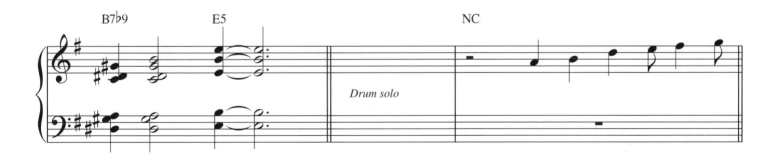

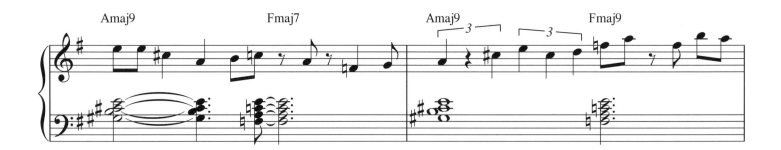

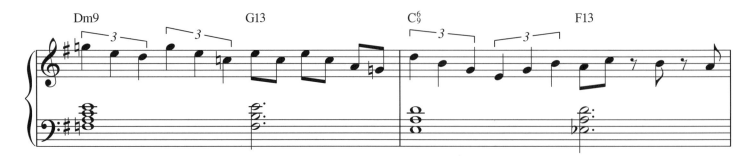

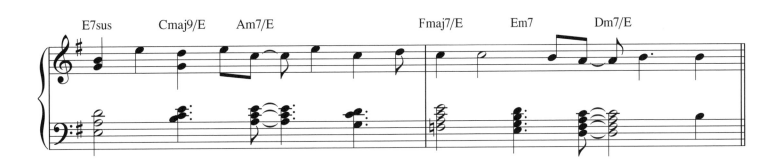

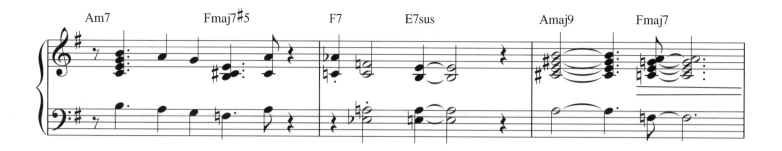

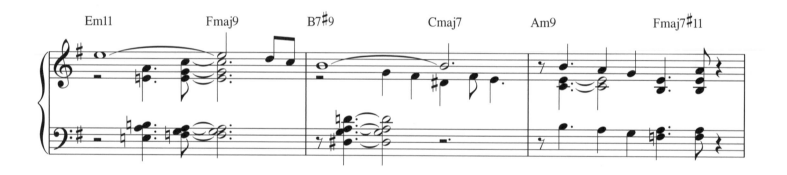

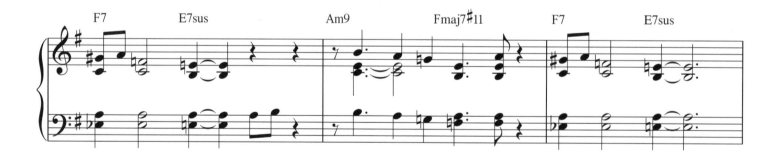

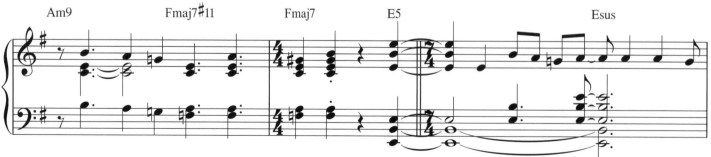

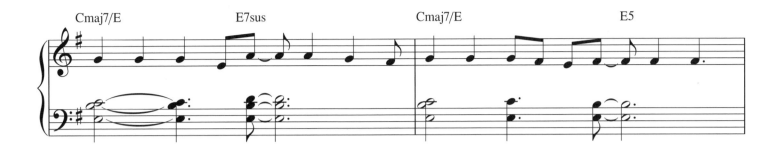

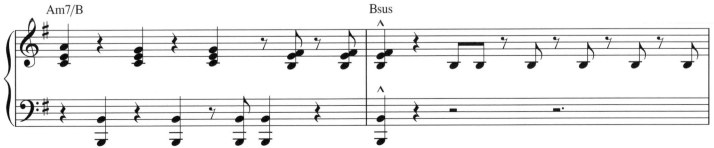

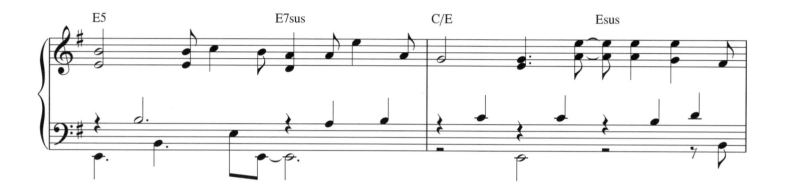

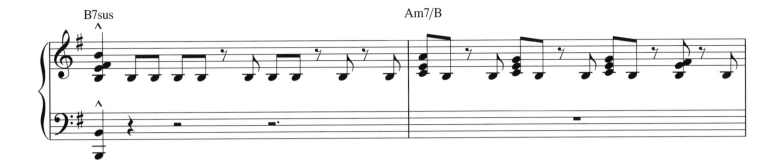

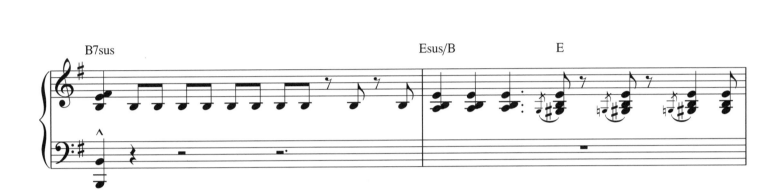

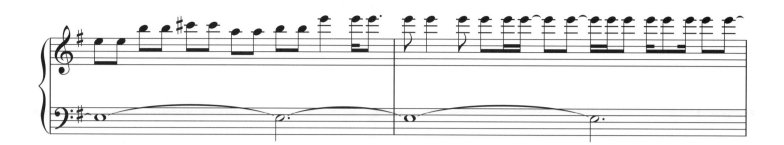

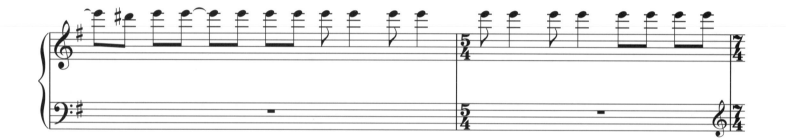

# Stella by Starlight

from the Paramount Picture THE UNINVITED

**Words by Ned Washington**
**Music by Victor Young**

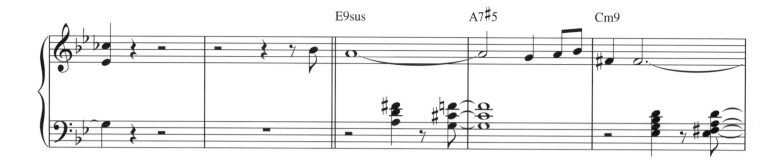

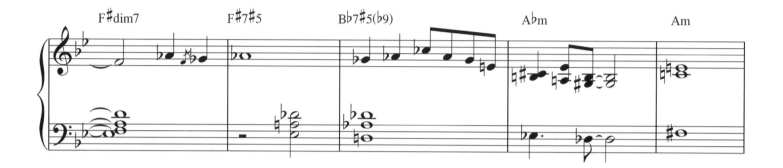

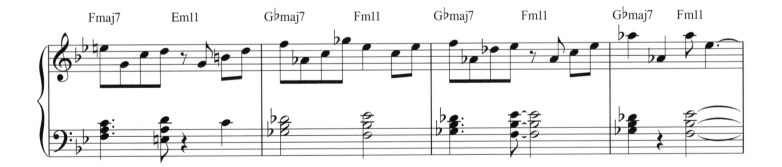

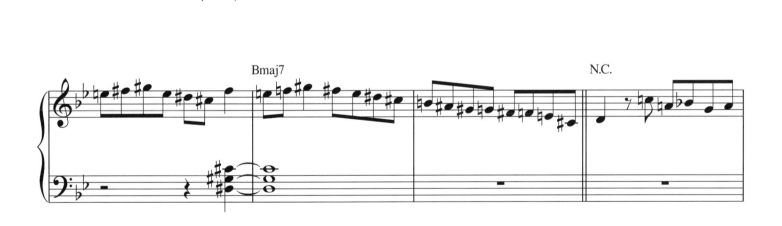

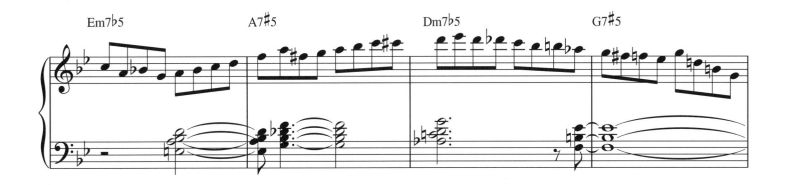

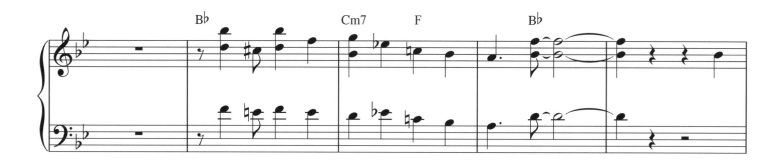

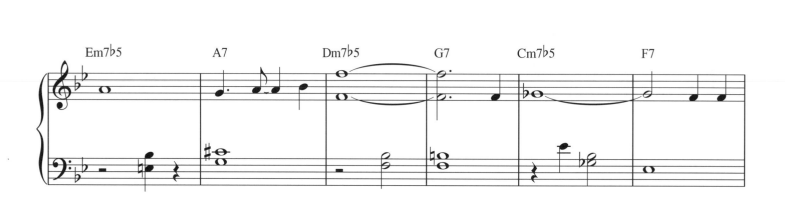

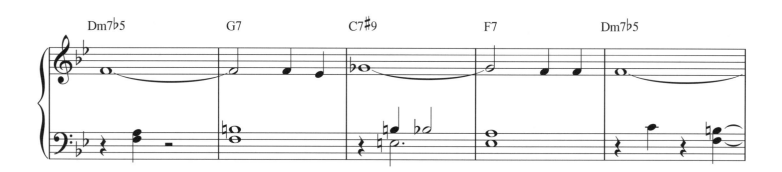

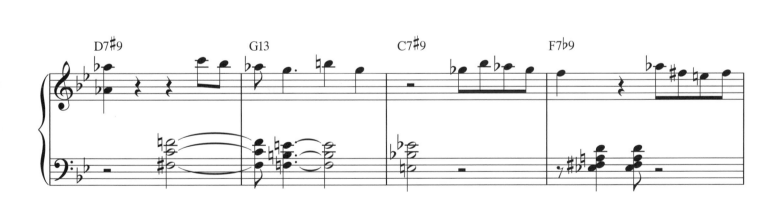

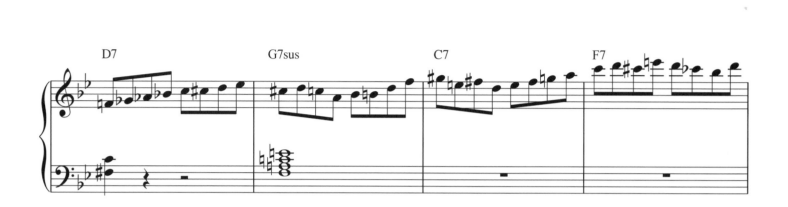

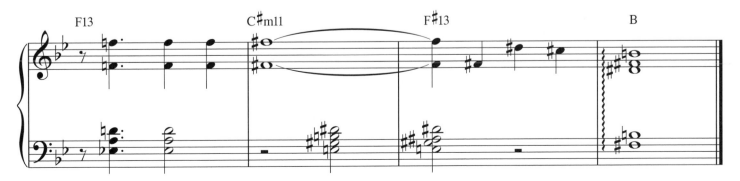

# There Will Never Be Another You

## from the Motion Picture ICELAND

**Words by Mack Gordon**
**Music by Harry Warren**

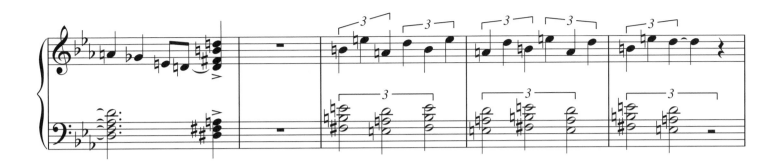

*Drum solo*

# With a Song in My Heart

## from SPRING IS HERE

**Words by Lorenz Hart**
**Music by Richard Rodgers**

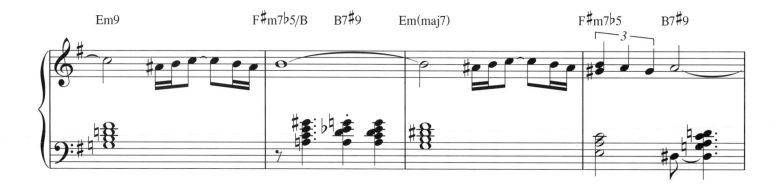

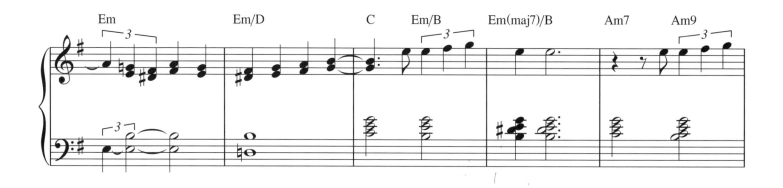

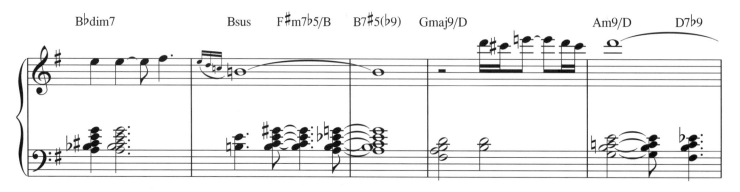

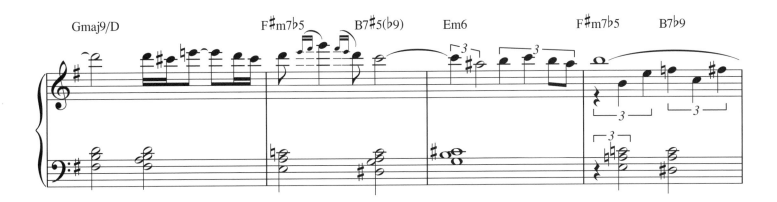

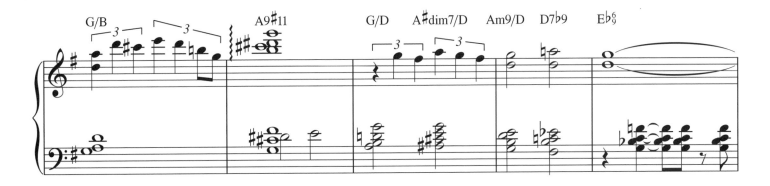

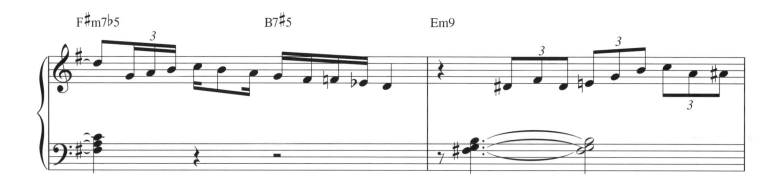

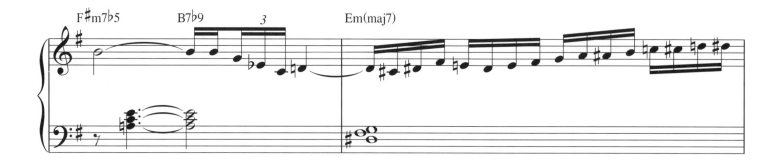

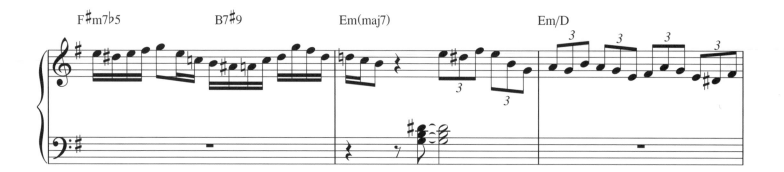

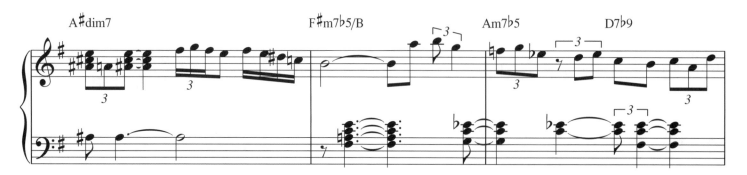

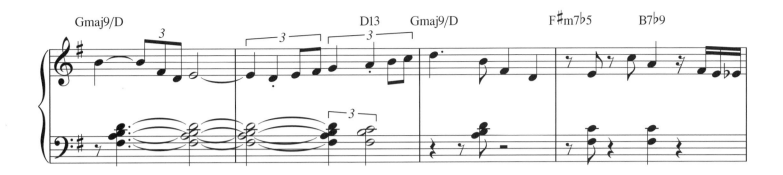

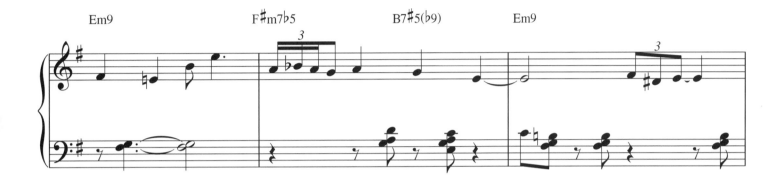

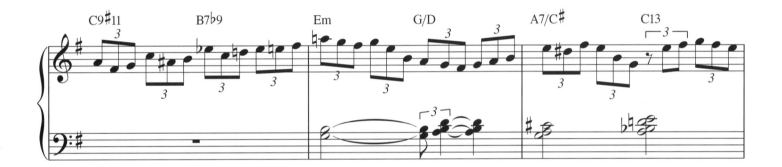

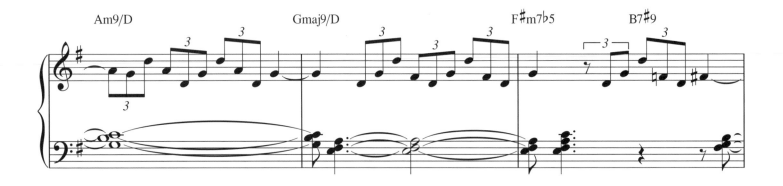

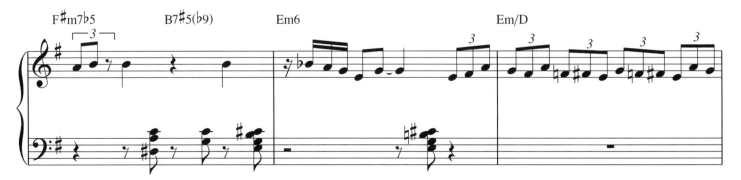

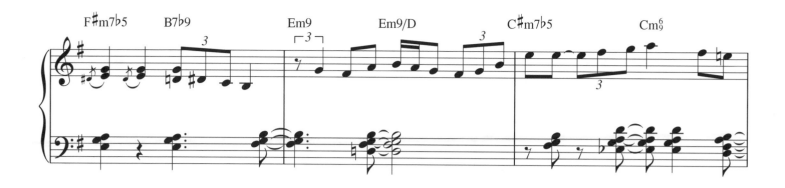

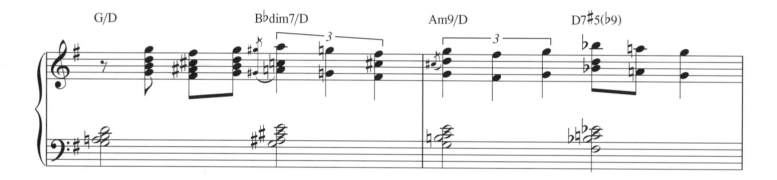

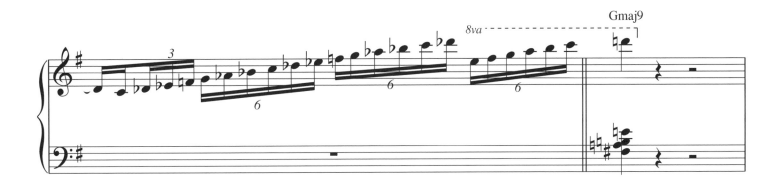

**Swing**

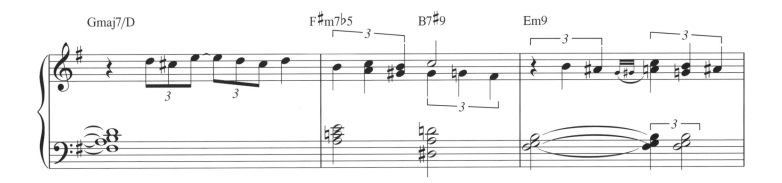

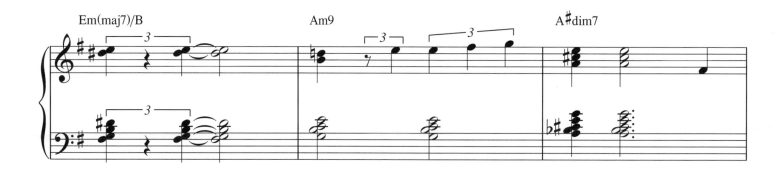

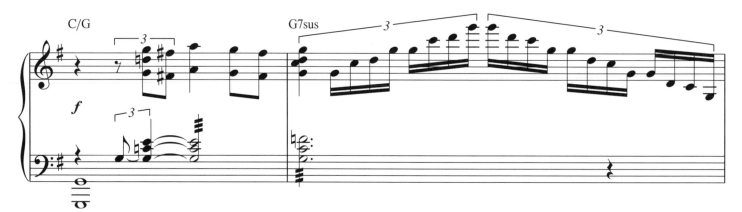

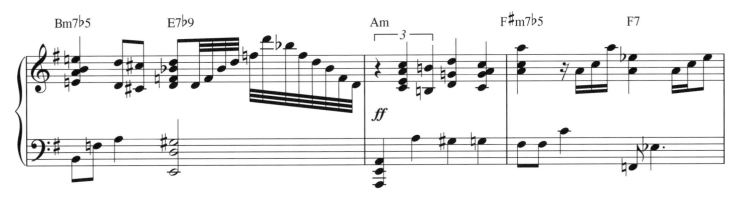

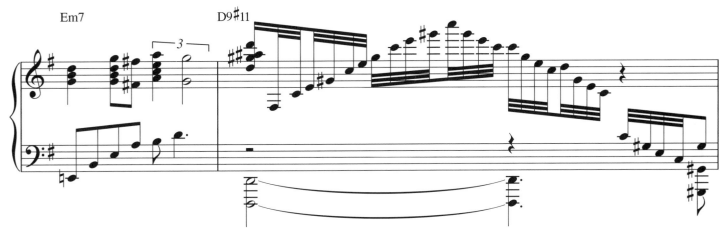

**In time, Bossa**

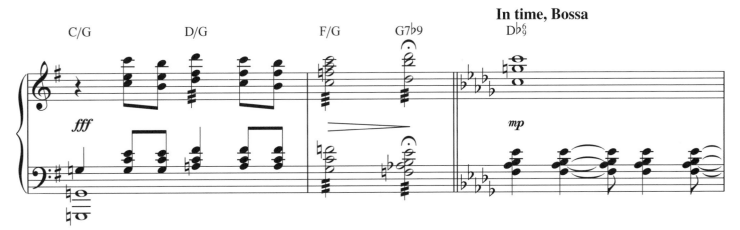

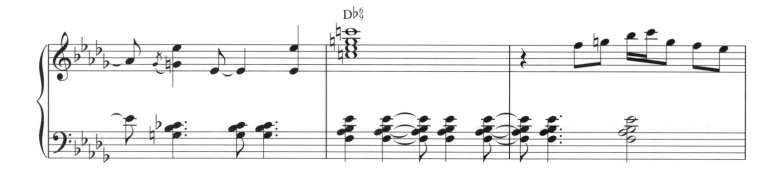

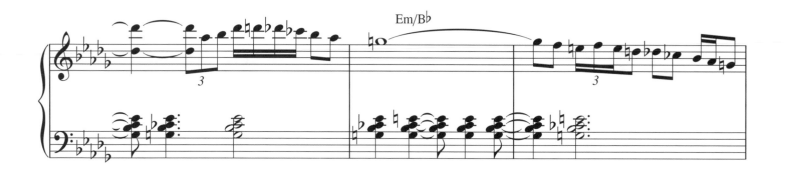

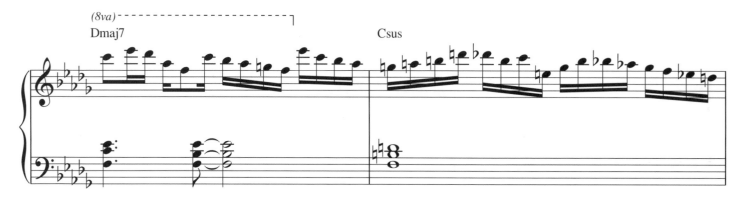

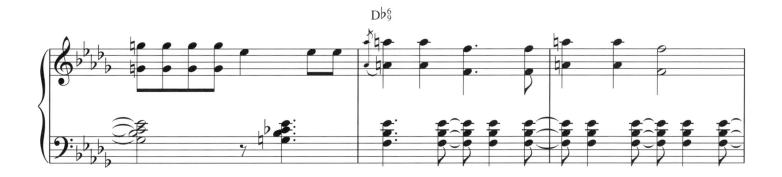

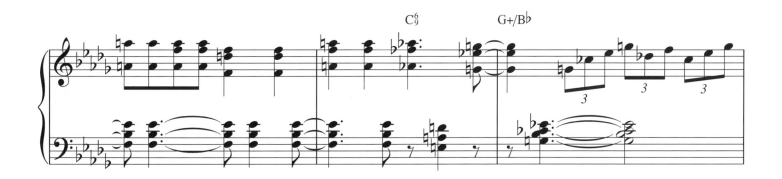

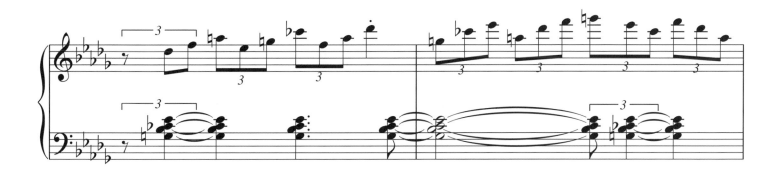

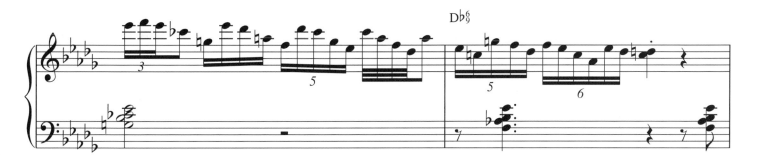

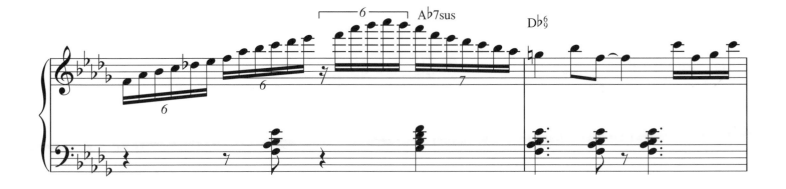

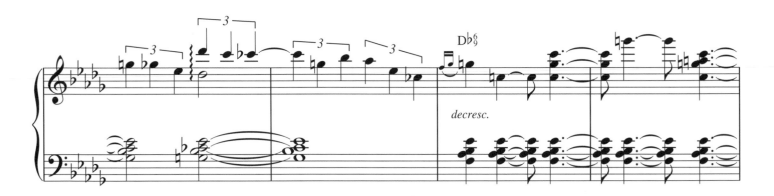

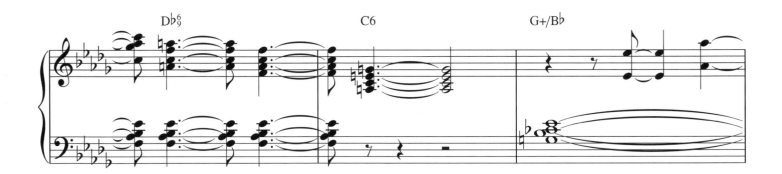

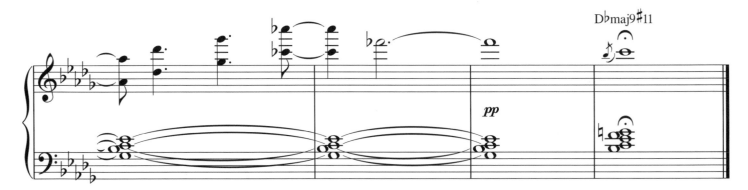

# DISCOGRAPHY

**All the Things You Are** – *Live at Visiones* (Concord Jazz-4675)

**Autumn Leaves** – *Alex Riel: Celebration* (Stunt-00232)

**Blue in Green** – *Live at Visiones* (Concord Jazz-4675)

**Ivoronics** – *A Delicate Balance* (RCA Victor-51694)

**Little Appetites** – *Beauty Secrets* (RCA Victor-69904)

**My Funny Valentine** – *Form and Fantasy Vol. 1* (Doubletime Jazz-186)

**Nardis** – *Form and Fantasy Vol. 1* (Doubletime Jazz-186)

**Stella by Starlight** – *Live at Visiones* (Concord Jazz-4675)

**There Will Never Be Another You** – *Live at Visiones* (Concord Jazz-4675)

**With a Song in My Heart** – *Beauty Secrets* (RCA Victor-69904)